Arabic Phrases, Sayings & Idioms
Fast Arabic to Enrich your Language Now

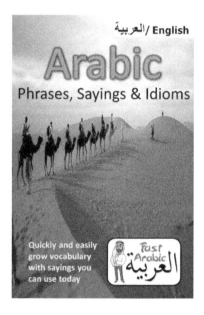

The fastest resources available to grow your Arabic vocabulary now!

Bilingual Edition
Arabic/English Side-by-Side

Fast Arabic Series

www.FastArabic.com

Copyright © 2017 by Fast Arabic

Table

Introduction

Welcome to the fastest resources available to grow your Arabic vocabulary now. This bilingual book attempts to identify the most easily accessible, high frequency Arabic sayings to enhance your language in the fastest way possible. Historically, the Middle East is the cradle of civilization in the world. The cultural heritage is amazing. The Arabic language is the key to unlocking the secrets and wisdom of the ancient past. It is also the window into current trends and modern ideas.

In this deluxe bilingual edition, learn the most common and high frequency Arabic sayings, idioms and phrases. These sayings will boost your language skills, and instantly build rapport and understanding with native Arabic speakers.

In fact, many of these ideas span across foreign cultures, and manifest shared human experiences. Because Arabic culture is particularly long, there are hundreds and thousands of sayings. This book will focus on the high frequency sayings that are shared across the Arabic speaking world, regardless of dialect.

Students that are beginning to learn Arabic can use these sayings as a bridge to quickly build a foundation of phrases to use in their studies and initial conversations. Instructors can use these to inspire confidence and progress in their students. The more advanced students can most quickly absorb the lists, enhancing their vocabulary by scores of high frequency phrases in record time.

Students traditionally discover these sayings one by one during classes and study. Now with *Arabic Phrases, Sayings & Idioms* you can rapidly speed up learning significantly.

Fast Arabic

www.FastArabic.com

Pronunciation Guide

ا	ā	long \<a\> sound like in the word "sad"
ب	b	\<b\> sound in the word "bread"
ت	t	\<t\> sound in "tennis" or "terrific"
ث	th	\<th\> sound in "three"
ج	j	\<j\> sound in the word "James"
ح	H	deeper \<H\> sound from throat, like in the word "Horace"
خ	kh	made at top of throat, the \<kh\> sound in "lochness monster"
د	d	\<d\> sound, as in the word "doctor"
ذ	dh	the \<th\> sound in "that", almost like a "dh" sound
ر	r	the \<r\> sound in "rapid", and often rolled like Spanish
ز	z	\<z\> like the word "zebra"
س	s	\<s\> like the word "silly"
ش	sh	\<sh\> like the word "should"
ص	S	deeper \<S\> sound, like the word "sun" or "saw"
ض	D	deeper \<D\> sound, like the sound from "dawd"
ط	T	deeper \<T\> sound, like the sound from "taught"
ظ	DH	deeper \<DH\> sound, like the sound from "thy" or "thou"
ع	ʿ	the \<ein\> sound, like the beginning of the word "Einstein"
غ	gh	same as \<ein\>, except with gargle sound "Gh-Einstein"
ف	f	\<f\> as in "Frank"
ق	q	\<q\> sound like the word "queen"
ك	k	\<k\> sound in the word "kabob"
ل	l	\<l\> sound in the word "lamb"
م	m	\<m\> sound in the word "mat"
ن	n	\<n\> sound in the word "night"
ه	h	\<h\> sound in the word "hat"
و	w	when short, \<w\> sound in the word "witch"
و	ū	when long, \<oo\> sound word "zoom"
ي	y	when short, \<y\> sound in the word "yes"
ي	I	when long, \<ee\> sound in the word "bee"
ء	'	glottal stop, like the 'uh' sound in 'uh oh'

1. We are in the Same Boat

نحن في الهوا سوا

Nahnu fii al-huwa sua

The Arabic translation conveys the idea that "we all are in the same air." The saying means that people are facing a shared situation.

2. History Repeats Itself

التاريخ يعيد نفسه

al-taarik y3eed nefsahu

The same kinds of events appear to repeat throughout history. We are either fortunate to learn the lessons from history, or we are often bound to repeat the same mistakes of our ancestors.

3. Speaking is one thing, doing is another

الكلام شيء و الفعل شيء ثاني

al-kalaam shay' wa al-f3l shay' thaanee

Talk is cheap, and words are quick to be spoken.
Taking action is more difficult.

4. Merely Words

kalaam fii kalaam

Words are often not followed up with action. When someone is blowing hot air or proposing an idea, there is often no action that follows.

5. Enemy of my Enemy is my Friend

عدو عدوي صديقي

3du 3duwi sadiqi

Two different parties can or should work together against a common enemy.

6. Every Action has a Reaction

لكل فعل رد فعل

li-kul f3l radd f3l

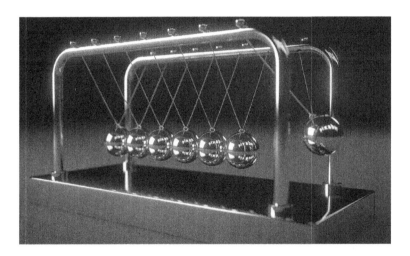

Newton's third law: For every action, there is an equal and opposite reaction. The statement means that in everyinteraction, there is a pair of forces acting on the two interacting objects.

7. In your dream / When Pigs Fly

بالحلم

bil helam

بالمشمش

bil mishmish

A way of saying that something will never happen. The first phrase means "in your dreams", the second "in apricots". Both mean the same thing.

8. One day like honey, another like Onion

يوم عسل و يوم بصل

yom 3sl wa yom basl

Some days are good, and others bad.

9. Patience is Key to Victory

الصبر مفتاح الفرج

al-sabr maftaH al-farj

Good things come to those that wait. Patience can lead to great results.

10. In the Long Run

في نهاية المطاف

fii nihyat al-maTaaf

At the end of the day, in conclusion...

11. Between a Rock and a Hard Place

بين نارين

bayn narane

Caught between two horrible situations...

12. Every New Language, a New Person

كل لسان بأنسان

kul lisan bi-ansan

Speaking a new language opens a new world of possibilities for someone.

13. Time is Like a Sword, Use it or Get Cut

الوقت كالسيف ان لم تقطعه قطعك

al-waqt kal-sayf in lem teqaT3hu qaT3k

Time waits for no man. We can use time wisely, or face the consequences of wasting it.

14. Judge a Book by its Cover

الكتاب يبين من عنوانه

al-kitaab yubayn min 3nwanih

Often we are taught that you cannot judge a book by its cover. However, common sense tells us that judging by the cover is often an effective method.

15. A Friend in need is a friend Indeed

الصديق وقت الضيق

al-sadiq waqt al-diq

A person who helps at a difficult time is a true friend.

16. Still Waters Run Deep

تحت السواهي دواهي

tahat al-suwahi duwahi

A quiet or reserved manner may conceal a more passionate nature.

17. All Roads Lead to Rome

كل الدروب تؤدي إلى روما

kul al-durub tuadee illa ruma

There are many different ways to reach the same outcome or destination.

18. In the Immediate Future

في القريب العاجل

fii al-qareeb al-3ajil

19. The More the Merrier

كلما زاد العدد كلما زاد المرح

kulema zaad al-3did kulema zaad al-maraH

20. The Pen is the Mightiest Weapon

القلم هو أقوى سلاح

al-qilam huwa aqwaa salaH

21. Add Fuel to the Fire

زاد الطين بلة

zad al-tina bila

وضع البنزين على النار

wad3 al-benzeen 3la al-nar

The first Arabic phrase literally means to pile on more dirt. The second phrase is more a direct translation.

22. In Name Only (no actions taken)

بالاسم فقط

bil-ism faqat

By description, but not in reality.

23. Satan Only is Strange

ما غريب الا الشيطان

ma ghreeb illa al-shaytan

Means that the situation or thing is not that strange, and that only Satan is strange.

24. No more Tricks up your Sleeve; helpless

ما في اليد حيلة

ma fii al-yed hila

All out of tricks and options. Helpness, and in need of support.

25. Up One Day and Down the Next

يوم لك و يوم عليك

yom lak wa yom 3layk

What goes up, must come down. Riding high one day, and down the next.

26. Absent Party is not to Blame

الغايب عذره معه

al-ghayib 3dhrah m3h

Give someone the benefit of the doubt, until you hear out their explanation.

27. Drowning Man will Catch at a Straw

الغريق بيتعلق بقشاية

al-ghariq bi-yet3laq bi-qishaya

A person in desperation will grasp at anything for help.

28. Carrot and Stick Policy

سياسة العصا و الجزرة

siasat al-3sa wa al-jazra

Rewards and punishments to create incentives.

29. Preparations in Full Swing

الاستعدادت تجري على قدم و ساق

al-ast3dadat tajri 3la qadam wa saq

30. Curiosity Killed the Cat

من تدخل في مالا يعنيه
نال مالا يرضيه

min tedakhul fii mala y3nih nal mala yurdih

Be cautious when poking your nose in other's affairs.

31. Unity is Strength

الاتحاد قوة

al-atihad qua

32. The Smarter you Get, the Less you Speak

إذا تم العقل نقص الكلام

idha tama al-3ql naqs al-kalaam

33. All that Glitters is not Gold

ما كُلُّ ما يَلْمَعُ ذَهَبا

ma kul ma yalm3 dhahaban

Not everything that looks precious or true turns out to be so.

34. Strike while the Iron is Hot

اطرق الحديد وهو حار

atraq al-Hadeed huwa Har

Make use of an opportunity immediately when it presents itself.

35. Forbidden Fruit is Sweet

كل ممنوع مرغوب

kul memnu3 marghub

Things can become attractive or desirable partly because they are illegal or immoral.

36. Birds of a Feather Flock Together

الطيور على اشكالها تقع

al-Tiyur 3la ashkaliha taq3

People of the same sort, tastes and interests will be found together.

37. Bird in the Hand worth Two in the Bush

عصفور في اليد خير من عشرة على الشجرة

3sfur fii al-yed khayr min 3shrat 3la al-shejra

Better to hold onto something one has than to risk losing it by trying to get something better.

38. Diamond Cut Diamond

لايفلُ الحديد إلا الحديد

layafalu al-hadid illa alhadid

A situation in which an able person meets their match.

39. Easy Come, Easy Go

ما يأتي بسهولة يذهب بسهولة

ma yati basahula yadhhab basahula

Something acquired without effort may be abandoned or lost casually and without regret.

40. Make a Mountain out of a Mole Hill

يعمل من الحَبّة قُبّة

y3ml min al-habba qabba

In Arabic this translates as making a dome out of a grain of sand. Over-reactive, histrionic behaviour where a person makes too much of a minor issue.

41. Life is Sweet

الحياة حلوة

al-hayat helua

42. No Smoke without Fire

لا دخان بلا نار

la dukhan bila nar

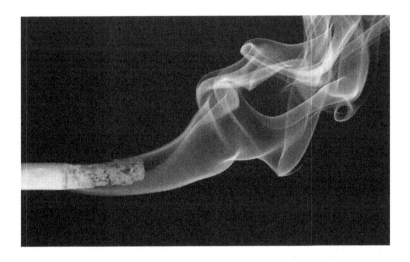

There's always some reason for a rumor.

43. Everything is Possible in this World

كل شيء ممكن في هذا
العالم

kul shay' mumkin fii hadha al-3lm

44. Nothing New Under the Sun

لا جديد تحت الشمس

la jaded tahat al-shems

Everything has been seen before.

45. World wasn't Created in a Day

لم تخلق الدنيا في يوم

lem tekhluq al-dunya fii yom

Rome wasn't built in a day, and neither was the world. Great things take time to create.

46. The Sea has Fish for Everyone

في البحر رزق للجميع

fii al-bahar razq lil-jami3

The world has enough for everyone.

47. Cross the Stream where it is Shallow

امشي شهر و لا تعبر نهر

amshee shahr wa la t3bir nahr

Do things in the easiest possible way.

48. Speak of the Devil (and he appears)

جبنا سيرة القط جه ينط

jabana sirat al-qaT J

An object of discussion unexpectedly becomes present during the conversation.

49. The Stick to those that Disobey

العصا لمن عصا

al-3sa liman 3sa

50. Every Dog has their Day

لكل ظالم نهاية

li-kul Dhalim nihaya

Everyone will have good luck or success at some point in their lives.

51. The Ends Justify the Means

الغاية تبرر الوسيلة

al-ghaya tubarir al-wasila

A good outcome excuses any wrongs committed to attain it.

52. To Break a Long Fast with an Onion

صام صام و فطر على بصلة

sam sam wa fatur 3la basila

To wait patiently, only to have a bad outcome.

53. The Promise of a Freeman is a Debt

وعد الحر دَين عليه

wa3d al-hurr din 3layh

A promise creates a debt that we cannot forget.

54. Fair Face Hiding a Foul Heart

من بره هلله هلله ومن
جوه يعلم الله

min barah hallah hallah wa min juh ye3lm
Allah

55. Ebb and Flow

مد و جزر

mad wa juzur

A recurrent or rhythmical pattern of coming and going or decline and regrowth.

56. A Honey Tongue, a Heart of Gall

في الوجه مراية وفي القفا سلاية

fii al-wajh miraya wa fii al-qafa salaya

57. When the Cat is Away, the Mice will Play

إن غاب القط، العب يا فار

inna ghab al-qatta, al-3b ya-far

People will naturally take advantage of the absence of someone in authority to do as they like.

58. You cannot make a Crab Walk Straight

ذيل الكلب عمره ما يتعدل

dhil al-kalb 3mruh ma ta3dal

Some things are not possible. Attempting them will only cause frustration.

59. Other Times, Other Manners

لكل حادث حديث

li-kul haadith hadeeth

Different generations or eras have different customs.

60. Living with Cripples you Learn to Limp

من عاشر القوم أربعين يوما صار منهم

min 3shr al-qawm 'arb3in yoman Sar minhum

61. A Word is Enough to the Wise

العاقل تكفيه الاشارة

al-3aqil takafih al-'shara

Wise people can take hints; they don't need to have everything explained to them at great length.

62. A Fox is not Taken Twice in the Same Snare

لا يلدغ المؤمن من جحر مرتين

la yuldigh alm'min min jahr maratayn

63. Scapegoat

كبش الفداء

kabash al-fada'

64. Marriage of Convenience

zawaj maslaha

A marriage that is arranged for practical, financial, or political reasons.

65. Topsy Turvy; Turned Upside Down

قلب الامور راسا على عقب

qalb al-'amur rasaan 3la 3qib

Chaos, disturbance or all backwards.

66. Like Clockwork

مثل الساعة

methyl al-sa3a

67. Piece of Cake (Easy)

سهل مثل الماء

sahl methyl al-ma'

In Arabic, this is translated as "easy as water".

68. Over my Dead Body

على جثتي

3la juthatee

Used to emphasize that one opposes something
and would do anything to prevent it from
happening.

69. Blue Blood; People of Good Background

ابن ناس

ibn nas

70. At the End of Nowhere

في اخر الدنيا

fii ackr al-dunia

In a very distant or remote place. Translates as "in another world".

71. Turn over a New Leaf

فتح صفحة جديدة

fataH safha jadeeda

In Arabic, this means to turn over a new page. To begin again, fresh; to reform and begin again.

72. In the Blink of an Eye

في لمح البصر

fii lamah al-basar

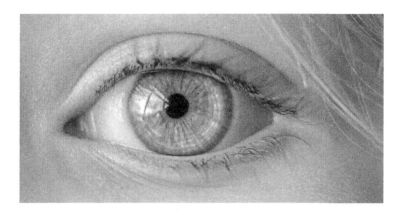

Extremely quickly.

73. Beat Around the Bush

يلف و يدور

yeluf wa yadur

To avoid answering a question; to stall; to waste time.

74. Practice Makes Perfect

التكرار يعلّم الحمار

al-tekrar y3llm al-hamar

In Arabic, repetition teaches the donkey.

For additional resources visit

www.FastArabic.com